® 2016 apostle Arne Horn

{Series}
Fathers of the Second Century:

The treatise of Athenagoras

The Athenian, Philosopher and Christian, on the Resurrection of the Dead.
Book II

This is a publication of the New Apostolic Bible Covenant®

I.S.B.N.: 978-1-326-79527-6
©2016 N.A.B.C.
Design cover: @postle Arne
Source cover photo:
http://minzscanvas.yolasite.com/resources/IMG_8820.JPG
https://www.lulu.com/spotlight/almere2010
Twitter: https://twitter.com/ApostleArne

No part of this publication may be reproduced and / or published by print, photocopy, microfilm, Internet or by any means without permission of the author / publisher!
Disclaimer: There can't be no rights derived from the texts in this Book. The used information are from encyclopedias and through research!

® 2016 apostle Arne Horn

Index:

® 2016 apostle Arne Horn

Introductory Note

Athenagoras (/ˌæθəˈnæɡərəs/; Greek: Ἀθηναγόρας ὁ Ἀθηναῖος; c. 133 – c. 190 AD) was a Father of the Church, an Ante-Nicene Christian-apologist who lived during the second half of the 2nd century of whom little is known for certain, besides that he was Athenian (though possibly not originally from Athens), a philosopher, and a convert to Christianity. In his writings he styles himself as *"Athenagoras, the Athenian, Philosopher, and Christian"*. There is some evidence that he was a Platonist before his conversion, but this is not certain.

® 2016 apostle Arne Horn

Chapter 1:1-11

Defence of the truth should precede discussions regarding it.

1. By the side of every opinion and doctrine which agrees with the truth of things, there springs up some falsehood; and it does so, not because it takes its rise naturally from some fundamental principle, or from some cause peculiar to the matter in hand, but because it is invented on purpose by men who set a value on the spurious seed, for its tendency to corrupt the truth.
2. This is apparent, in the first place, from those who in former times addicted themselves to such inquiries, and their want of agreement with their predecessors and contemporaries, and then, not least, from the very confusion which marks the discussions that are now going on.
3. For such men have left no truth free from their calumnious attacks—not the being of God, not His knowledge, not His operations, not those books which follow by a regular and strict sequence from these, and delineate for us the doctrines of piety.
4. On the contrary, some of them utterly, and once for all, give up in despair the truth concerning these things, and some distort it to suit their own views, and some of set purpose doubt even of things which are palpably evident.
5. Hence I think that those who bestow attention on such subjects should adopt two lines of argument, one in defence of the truth, another concerning the truth: that in defence of the truth, for disbelievers and doubters; that concerning the truth, for such as are candid and receive the truth with readiness.
6. Accordingly it behoves those who wish to investigate these matters, to keep in view that which the necessity of the case in each instance requires, and to regulate their discussion by this; to accommodate the order of their treatment of these subjects to what is suitable to the occasion, and not for the sake of appearing always to preserve the same method, to disregard fitness and the place which properly belongs to each topic.
7. For, so far as proof and the natural order are concerned, dissertations concerning the truth always take precedence of those in defence of it; but, for the purpose of greater utility, the order must be reversed, and arguments in defence of it precede those concerning it.
8. For the farmer could not properly cast the seed into the

® 2016 apostle Arne Horn

ground, unless he first extirpated the wild wood, and whatever would be hurtful to the good seed; nor the physician introduce any wholesome medicines into the body that needed his care, if he did not previously remove the disease within, or stay that which was approaching.

9. Neither surely can he who wishes to teach the truth persuade any one by speaking about it, so long as there is a false opinion lurking in the mind of his hearers, and barring the entrance of his arguments.

10. And, therefore, from regard to greater utility, I myself sometimes place arguments in defence of the truth before those concerning the truth; and on the present occasion it appears to me, looking at the requirements of the case, not without advantage to follow the same method in treating of the resurrection.

11. For in regard to this subject also we find some utterly disbelieving, and some others doubting, and even among those who have accepted the first principles some who are as much at a loss what to believe as those who doubt; the most unaccountable thing of all being, that they are in this state of mind without having any ground whatsoever in the matters themselves for their disbelief, or finding it possible to assign any reasonable cause why they disbelieve or experience any perplexity.

 ® 2016 apostle Arne Horn

Chapter 2:1-9

A resurrection is not impossible.

1. Let us, then, consider the subject in the way I have indicated. If all disbelief does not arise from levity and inconsideration, but if it springs up in some minds on strong grounds and accompanied by the certainty which belongs to truth [*well and good*]; for it then maintains the appearance of being just, when the thing itself to which their disbelief relates appears to them unworthy of belief; but to disbelieve things which are not deserving of disbelief, is the act of men who do not employ a sound judgment about the truth.
2. It behoves, therefore, those who disbelieve or doubt concerning the resurrection, to form their opinion on the subject, not from any view they have hastily adopted, and from what is acceptable to profligate men, but either to assign the origin of men to no cause (*a notion which is very easily refuted*), or, ascribing the cause of all things to God, to keep steadily in view the principle involved in this article of belief, and from this to demonstrate that the resurrection is utterly unworthy of credit.
3. This they will succeed in, if they are able to show that it is either impossible for God, or contrary to His will, to unite and gather together again bodies that are dead, or even entirely dissolved into their elements, so as to constitute the same persons.
4. If they cannot do this, let them cease from this godless disbelief, and from this blasphemy against sacred things: for, that they do not speak the truth when they say that it is impossible, or not in accordance with the divine will, will clearly appear from what I am about to say.
5. A thing is in strictness of language considered impossible to a person, when it is of such a kind that he either does not know what is to be done, or has not sufficient power for the proper doing of the thing known.
6. For he who is ignorant of anything that requires to be done, is utterly unable either to attempt or to do what he is ignorant of; and he, too, who knows ever so well what has to be done, and by what means, and how, but either has no power at all to do the thing known, or not power sufficient, will not even make the attempt, if he be wise and consider his powers; and if he did attempt it without due consideration, he would not accomplish his purpose.
7. But it is not possible for God to be ignorant, either of the

® 2016 apostle Arne Horn

nature of the bodies that are to be raised, as regards both the members entire and the particles of which they consist, or whither each of the dissolved particles passes, and what part of the elements has received that which is dissolved and has passed into that with which it has affinity, although to men it may appear quite impossible that what has again combined according to its nature with the universe should be separable from it again.

8. For He from whom, antecedently to the peculiar formation of each, was not concealed either the nature of the elements of which the bodies of men were to consist, or the parts of these from which He was about to take what seemed to Him suitable for the formation of the human body, will manifestly, after the dissolution of the whole, not be ignorant whither each of the particles has passed which He took for the construction of each.

9. For, viewed relatively to the order of things now obtaining among us, and the judgment we form concerning other matters, it is a greater thing to know beforehand that which has not yet come to pass; but, viewed relatively to the majesty and wisdom of God, both are according to nature, and it is equally easy to know beforehand things that have not yet come into existence, and to know things which have been dissolved.

® 2016 apostle Arne Horn

Chapter 3:1-5

He who could create, can also raise up the dead.

1. Moreover also, that His power is sufficient for the raising of dead bodies, is shown by the creation of these same bodies. For if, when they did not exist, He made at their first formation the bodies of men, and their original elements, He will, when they are dissolved, in whatever manner that may take place, raise them again with equal ease: for this, too, is equally possible to Him.
2. And it is no damage to the argument, if some suppose the first beginnings to be from matter, or the bodies of men at least to be derived from the elements as the first materials, or from seed.
3. For that power which could give shape to what is regarded by them as shapeless matter, and adorn it, when destitute of form and order, with many and diverse forms, and gather into one the several portions of the elements, and divide the seed which was one and simple into many, and organize that which was unorganized, and give life to that which had no life,—that same power can reunite what is dissolved, and raise up what is prostrate, and restore the dead to life again, and put the corruptible into a state of incorruption.
4. And to the same Being it will belong, and to the same power and skill, to separate that which has been broken up and distributed among a multitude of animals of all kinds which are wont to have recourse to such bodies, and glut their appetite upon them,—to separate this, I say, and unite it again with the proper members and parts of members, whether it has passed into some one of those animals.
5. Or into many, or thence into others, or, after being dissolved along with these, has been carried back again to the original elements, resolved into these according to a natural law—a matter this which seems to have exceedingly confounded some, even of those admired for wisdom, who, I cannot tell why, think those doubts worthy of serious attention which are brought forward by the many.

 ® 2016 apostle Arne Horn

Chapter 4:1-4

Objection from the fact that some human bodies have become part of others.

1. These persons, to wit, say that many bodies of those who have come to an unhappy death in shipwrecks and rivers have become food for fishes, and many of those who perish in war, or who from some other sad cause or state of things are deprived of burial, lie exposed to become the food of any animals which may chance to light upon them.
2. Since, then, bodies are thus consumed, and the members and parts composing them are broken up and distributed among a great multitude of animals, and by means of nutrition become incorporated with the bodies of those that are nourished by them,—in the first place, they say, their separation from these is impossible; and besides this, in the second place, they adduce another circumstance more difficult still.
3. When animals of the kind suitable for human food, which have fed on the bodies of men, pass through their stomach, and become incorporated with the bodies of those who have partaken of them, it is an absolute necessity, they say, that the parts of the bodies of men which have served as nourishment to the animals which have partaken of them should pass into other bodies of men, since the animals which meanwhile have been nourished by them convey the nutriment derived from those by whom they were nourished into those men of whom they become the nutriment.
4. Then to this they tragically add the devouring of offspring perpetrated by people in famine and madness, and the children eaten by their own parents through the contrivance of enemies, and the celebrated Median feast, and the tragic banquet of Thyestes; and they add, moreover, other such like unheard-of occurrences which have taken place among Greeks and barbarians: and from these things they establish, as they suppose, the impossibility of the resurrection, on the ground that the same parts cannot rise again with one set of bodies, and with another as well; for that either the bodies of the former possessors cannot be reconstituted, the parts which composed them having passed into others, or that, these having been restored to the former, the bodies of the last possessors will come short.

® 2016 apostle Arne Horn

Chapter 5:1-6

Reference to the processes of digestion and nutrition.

1. But it appears to me that such persons, in the first place, are ignorant of the power and skill of Him that fashioned and regulates this universe, who has adapted to the nature and kind of each animal the nourishment suitable and correspondent to it, and has neither ordained that everything in nature shall enter into union and combination with every kind of body, nor is at any loss to separate what has been so united.
2. But grants to the nature of each several created being or thing to do or to suffer what is naturally suited to it, and sometimes also hinders and allows or forbids whatever He wishes, and for the purpose He wishes; and, moreover, that they have not considered the power and nature of each of the creatures that nourish or are nourished.
3. Otherwise they would have known that not everything which is taken for food under the pressure of outward necessity turns out to be suitable nourishment for the animal, but that some things no sooner come into contact with the plicatures of the stomach than they are wont to be corrupted
4. And are vomited or voided, or disposed of in some other way, so that not even for a little time do they undergo the first and natural digestion, much less become incorporated with that which is to be nourished.
5. As also, that not even everything which has been digested in the stomach and received the first change actually arrives at the parts to be nourished, since some of it loses its nutritive power even in the stomach, and some during the second change, and the digestion that takes place in the liver is separated and passes into something else which is destitute of the power to nourish; nay, that the change which takes place in the liver does not all issue in nourishment to men.
6. But the matter changed is separated as refuse according to its natural purpose; and that the nourishment which is left in the members and parts themselves that have to be nourished sometimes changes to something else, according as that predominates which is present in greater or less abundance, and is apt to corrupt or to turn into itself that which comes near it.

® 2016 apostle Arne Horn

Chapter 6:1-11

Everything that is useless or hurtful is rejected.

1. Since, therefore, great difference of nature obtains in all animals, and the very nourishment which is accordant with nature is varied to suit each kind of animal, and the body which is nourished; and as in the nourishment of every animal there is a threefold cleansing and separation.
2. It follows that whatever is alien from the nourishment of the animal must be wholly destroyed and carried off to its natural place, or change into something else, since it cannot coalesce with it; that the power of the nourishing body must be suitable to the nature of the animal to be nourished, and accordant with its powers.
3. And that this, when it has passed through the strainers appointed for the purpose, and been thoroughly purified by the natural means of purification, must become a most genuine addition to the substance,—the only thing, in fact, which any one calling things by their right names would call nourishment at all.
4. Because it rejects everything that is foreign and hurtful to the constitution of the animal nourished and that mass of superfluous food introduced merely for filling the stomach and gratifying the appetite.
5. This nourishment, no one can doubt, becomes incorporated with the body that is nourished, interwoven and blended with all the members and parts of members.
6. But that which is different and contrary to nature is speedily corrupted if brought into contact with a stronger power, but easily destroys that which is overcome by it, and is converted into hurtful humours and poisonous qualities, because producing nothing akin or friendly to the body which is to be nourished.
7. And it is a very clear proof of this, that in many of the animals nourished, pain, or disease, or death follows from these things, if, owing to a too keen appetite, they take in mingled with their food something poisonous and contrary to nature; which, of course, would tend to the utter destruction of the body to be nourished, since that which is nourished is nourished by substances akin to it and which accord with its nature, but is destroyed by those of a contrary kind.
8. If, therefore, according to the different nature of animals, different kinds of food have been provided suitable to their nature, and none of that which the animal may have taken,

® 2016 apostle Arne Horn

not even an accidental part of it, admits of being blended with the body which is nourished, but only that part which has been purified by an entire digestion.

9. And undergone a complete change for union with a particular body, and adapted to the parts which are to receive nourishment,—it is very plain that none of the things contrary to nature can be united with those bodies for which it is not a suitable and correspondent nourishment.

10. But either passes off by the bowels before it produces some other humour, crude and corrupted; or, if it continue for a longer time, produces suffering or disease hard to cure, destroying at the same time the natural nourishment, or even the flesh itself which needs nourishment.

11. But even though it be expelled at length, overcome by certain medicines, or by better food, or by the natural forces, it is not got rid of without doing much harm, since it bears no peaceful aspect towards what is natural, because it cannot coalesce with nature.

® 2016 apostle Arne Horn

Chapter 7:1-12

The resurrection-body different from the present.

1. Nay, suppose we were to grant that the nourishment coming from these things (let it be so called, as more accordant with the common way of speaking), although against nature, is yet separated and changed into some one of the moist or dry.
2. Or warm or cold, matters which the body contains, our opponents would gain nothing by the concession: for the bodies that rise again are reconstituted from the parts which properly belong to them, whereas no one of the things mentioned is such a part.
3. Nor has it the form or place of a part; nay, it does not remain always with the parts of the body which are nourished, or rise again with the parts that rise, since no longer does blood, or phlegm, or bile, or breath, contribute anything to the life.
4. Neither, again, will the bodies nourished then require the things they once required, seeing that, along with the want and corruption of the bodies nourished, the need also of those things by which they were nourished is taken away.
5. To this must be added, that if we were to suppose the change arising from such nourishment to reach as far as flesh, in that case too there would be no necessity that the flesh recently changed by food of that kind.
6. If it became united to the body of some other man, should again as a part contribute to the formation of that body, since neither the flesh which takes it up always retains what it takes, nor does the flesh so incorporated abide and remain with that to which it was added, but is subject to a great variety of changes.
7. At one time being dispersed by toil or care, at another time being wasted by grief or trouble or disease, and by the distempers arising from being heated or chilled, the humours which are changed with the flesh and fat not receiving the nourishment so as to remain what they are.
8. But while such are the changes to which the flesh is subject, we should find that flesh, nourished by food unsuited to it, suffers them in a much greater degree; now swelling out and growing fat by what it has received, and then again rejecting it in some way or other, and decreasing in bulk, from one or more of the causes already mentioned; and that that alone remains in the parts which is adapted to bind together
9. Or cover, or warm the flesh that has been chosen by nature, and adheres to those parts by which it sustains the life which

® 2016 apostle Arne Horn

is according to nature, and fulfils the labours of that life.

10. So that whether the investigation in which we have just been engaged be fairly judged of, or the objections urged against our position be conceded, in neither case can it be shown that what is said by our opponents is true.

11. Nor can the bodies of men ever combine with those of the same nature, whether at any time, through ignorance and being cheated of their perception by some one else, men have partaken of such a body, or of their own accord, impelled by want or madness, they have defiled themselves with the body of one of like form.

12. For we are very well aware that some brutes have human forms, or have a nature compounded of men and brutes, such as the more daring of the poets are accustomed to represent.

® 2016 apostle Arne Horn

Chapter 8:1-9

Human flesh not the proper or natural food of men.

1. But what need is there to speak of bodies not allotted to be the food of any animal, and destined only for a burial in the earth in honour of nature, since the Maker of the world has not alloted any animal whatsoever as food to those of the same kind, although some others of a different kind serve for food according to nature?
2. If, indeed, they are able to show that the flesh of men was alloted to men for food, there will be nothing to hinder its being according to nature that they should eat one another, just like anything else that is allowed by nature, and nothing to prohibit those who dare to say such things from regaling themselves with the bodies of their dearest friends as delicacies, as being especially suited to them, and to entertain their living friends with the same fare.
3. But if it be unlawful even to speak of this, and if for men to partake of the flesh of men is a thing most hateful and abominable, and more detestable than any other unlawful and unnatural food or act.
4. And if what is against nature can never pass into nourishment for the limbs and parts requiring it, and what does not pass into nourishment can never become united with that which it is not adapted to nourish,—then can the bodies of men never combine with bodies like themselves.
5. To which this nourishment would be against nature, even though it were to pass many times through their stomach, owing to some most bitter mischance; but, removed from the influence of the nourishing power.
6. And scattered to those parts of the universe again from which they obtained their first origin, they are united with these for as long a period of time as may be the lot of each; and, separated thence again by the skill and power of Him who has fixed the nature of every animal, and furnished it with its peculiar powers.
7. They are united suitably, each to each, whether they have been burnt up by fire, or rotted by water, or consumed by wild beasts, or by any other animals, or separated from the entire body and dissolved before the other parts.
8. And, being again united with one another, they occupy the same place for the exact construction and formation of the same body, and for the resurrection and life of that which was dead, or even entirely dissolved.

® 2016 apostle Arne Horn

9. To expatiate further, however, on these topics, is not suitable; for all men are agreed in their decision respecting them,— those at least who are not half brutes.

® 2016 apostle Arne Horn

Chapter 9:1-7

Absurdity of arguing from man's impotency.

1. As there are many things of more importance to the inquiry before us, I beg to be excused from replying for the present to those who take refuge in the works of men, and even the constructors of them, who are unable to make anew such of their works as are broken in pieces.
2. Or worn out by time, or otherwise destroyed, and then from the analogy of potters and carpenters attempt to show that God neither can will, nor if He willed would be able, to raise again a body that is dead, or has been dissolved,—not considering that by such reasoning they offer the grossest insult to God.
3. Putting, as they do, on the same level the capabilities of things which are altogether different, or rather the natures of those who use them, and comparing the works of art with those of nature.
4. To bestow any serious attention on such arguments would be not undeserving of censure, for it is really foolish to reply to superficial and trifling objections.
5. It is surely far more probable, yea, most absolutely true, to say that what is impossible with men is possible with God.
6. And if by this statement of itself as probable, and by the whole investigation in which we have just been engaged reason shows it to be possible, it is quite clear that it is not impossible.
7. No, nor is it such a thing as God could not will.

® 2016 apostle Arne Horn

Chapter 10:1-9

It cannot be shown that God does not will a resurrection.

1. For that which is not accordant with His will is so either as being unjust or as unworthy of Him.
2. And again, the injustice regards either him who is to rise again, or some other than he. But it is evident that no one of the beings exterior to him, and that are reckoned among the things that have existence, is injured.
3. Spiritual natures (νοηταὶ φύσεις) cannot be injured by the resurrection of men, for the resurrection of men is no hindrance to their existing, nor is any loss or violence inflicted on them by it; nor, again, would the nature of irrational or inanimate beings sustain wrong, for they will have no existence after the resurrection, and no wrong can be done to that which is not.
4. But even if any one should suppose them to exist for ever, they would not suffer wrong by the renewal of human bodies: for if now, in being subservient to the nature of men and their necessities while they require them, and subjected to the yoke and every kind of drudgery, they suffer no wrong, much more, when men have become immortal and free from want.
5. And no longer need their service, and when they are themselves liberated from bondage, will they suffer no wrong. For if they had the gift of speech, they would not bring against the Creator the charge of making them, contrary to justice, inferior to men because they did not share in the same resurrection.
6. For to creatures whose nature is not alike the Just Being does not assign a like end. And, besides, with creatures that have no notion of justice there can be no complaint of injustice. Nor can it be said either that there is any injustice done as regards the man to be raised, for he consists of soul and body, and he suffers no wrong as to either soul or body.
7. No person in his senses will affirm that his soul suffers wrong, because, in speaking so, he would at the same time be unawares reflecting on the present life also; for if now, while dwelling in a body subject to corruption and suffering, it has had no wrong done to it, much less will it suffer wrong when living in conjunction with a body which is free from corruption and suffering.
8. The body, again, suffers no wrong; for if no wrong is done to it now while united a corruptible thing with an incorruptible, manifestly will it not be wronged when united an incorruptible

® 2016 apostle Arne Horn

with an incorruptible.

9. No; nor can any one say that it is a work unworthy of God to raise up and bring together again a body which has been dissolved: for if the worse was not unworthy of Him, namely, to make the body which is subject to corruption and suffering, much more is the better not unworthy, to make one not liable to corruption or suffering.

 ® 2016 apostle Arne Horn

Chapter 11:1-13

Recapitulation.

1. If, then, by means of that which is by nature first and that which follows from it, each of the points investigated has been proved, it is very evident that the resurrection of dissolved bodies is a work which the Creator can perform, and can will, and such as is worthy of Him.
2. For by these considerations the falsehood of the contrary opinion has been shown, and the absurdity of the position taken by disbelievers.
3. For why should I speak of their correspondence each with each, and of their connection with one another? If indeed we ought to use the word connection, as though they were separated by some difference of nature; and not rather say, that what God can do He can also will, and that what God can will it is perfectly possible for Him to do, and that it is accordant with the dignity of Him who wills it.
4. That to discourse concerning the truth is one thing, and to discourse in defence of it is another, has been sufficiently explained in the remarks already made, as also in what respects they differ from each other, and when and in dealing with whom they are severally useful.
5. But perhaps there is no reason why, with a view to the general certainty, and because of the connection of what has been said with what remains, we should not make a fresh beginning from these same points and those which are allied to them.
6. To the one kind of argument it naturally pertains to hold the foremost place, to the other to attend upon the first, and clear the way, and to remove whatever is obstructive or hostile.
7. The discourse concerning the truth, as being necessary to all men for certainty and safety, holds the first place, whether in nature, or order, or usefulness: in nature, as furnishing the knowledge of the subject; in order, as being in those things and along with those things which it informs us of; in usefulness, as being a guarantee of certainty and safety to those who become acquainted with it.
8. The discourse in defence of the truth is inferior in nature and force, for the refutation of falsehood is less important than the establishment of truth; and second in order, for it employs its strength against those who hold false opinions, and false opinions are an after growth from another sowing and from degeneration.

® 2016 apostle Arne Horn

9. But, notwithstanding all this, it is often placed first, and sometimes is found more useful, because it removes and clears away beforehand the disbelief which disquiets some minds, and the doubt or false opinion of such as have but recently come over.

10. And yet each of them is referrible to the same end, for the refutation of falsehood and the establishment of truth both have piety for their object: not, indeed, that they are absolutely one and the same, but the one is necessary, as I have said, to all who believe, and to those who are concerned about the truth and their own salvation; but the other proves to be more useful on some occasions, and to some persons, and in dealing with some.

11. Thus much by way of recapitulation, to recall what has been already said.

12. We must now pass on to what we proposed, and show the truth of the doctrine concerning the resurrection, both from the cause itself, according to which, and on account of which, the first man and his posterity were created, although they were not brought into existence in the same manner.

13. And from the common nature of all men as men; and further, from the judgment of their Maker upon them according to the time each has lived, and according to the rules by which each has regulated his behaviour,—a judgment which no one can doubt will be just.

® 2016 apostle Arne Horn

Chapter 12:1-20

Argument for the resurrection from the purpose contemplated in man's creation.

1. The argument from the cause will appear, if we consider whether man was made at random and in vain, or for some purpose; and if for some purpose, whether simply that he might live and continue in the natural condition in which he was created, or for the use of another.
2. And if with a view to use, whether for that of the Creator Himself, or of some one of the beings who belong to Him, and are by Him deemed worthy of greater care.
3. Now, if we consider this in the most general way, we find that a person of sound mind, and who is moved by a rational judgment to do anything, does nothing in vain which he does intentionally, but either for his own use.
4. Or for the use of some other person for whom he cares, or for the sake of the work itself, being moved by some natural inclination and affection towards its production.
5. For instance (*to make use of an illustration, that our meaning may be clear*), a man makes a house for his own use, but for cattle and camels and other animals of which he has need he makes the shelter suitable for each of them; not for his own use, if we regard the appearance only, though for that, if we look at the end he has in view, but as regards the immediate object, from concern for those for whom he cares.
6. He has children, too, not for his own use, nor for the sake of anything else belonging to him, but that those who spring from him may exist and continue as long as possible, thus by the succession of children and grandchildren comforting himself respecting the close of his own life, and hoping in this way to immortalize the mortal.
7. Such is the procedure of men. But God can neither have made man in vain, for He is wise, and no work of wisdom is in vain; nor for His own use, for He is in want of nothing.
8. But to a Being absolutely in need of nothing, no one of His works can contribute anything to His own use. Neither, again, did He make man for the sake of any of the other works which He has made.
9. For nothing that is endowed with reason and judgment has been created, or is created, for the use of another, whether greater or less than itself, but for the sake of the life and continuance of the being itself so created.
10. For reason cannot discover any use which might be deemed a

® 2016 apostle Arne Horn

cause for the creation of men, since immortals are free from want, and in need of no help from men in order to their existence; and irrational beings are by nature in a state of subjection.

11. And perform those services for men for which each of them was intended, but are not intended in their turn to make use of men: for it neither was nor is right to lower that which rules and takes the lead to the use of the inferior, or to subject the rational to the irrational, which is not suited to rule.

12. Therefore, if man has been created neither without cause and in vain (*for none of God's works is in vain, so far at least as the purpose of their Maker is concerned*), nor for the use of the Maker Himself, or of any of the works which have proceeded from Him.

13. It is quite clear that although, according to the first and more general view of the subject, God made man for Himself, and in pursuance of the goodness and wisdom which are conspicuous throughout the creation, yet, according to the view which more nearly touches the beings created, He made him for the sake of the life of those created, which is not kindled for a little while and then extinguished.

14. For to creeping things, I suppose, and birds, and fishes, or, to speak more generally, all irrational creatures, God has assigned such a life as that; but to those who bear upon them the image of the Creator Himself, and are endowed with understanding, and blessed with a rational judgment.

15. The Creator has assigned perpetual duration, in order that, recognising their own Maker, and His power and skill, and obeying law and justice, they may pass their whole existence free from suffering, in the possession of those qualities with which they have bravely borne their preceding life, although they lived in corruptible and earthly bodies.

16. For whatever has been created for the sake of something else, when that has ceased to be for the sake of which it was created, will itself also fitly cease to be, and will not continue to exist in vain, since, among the works of God, that which is useless can have no place.

17. But that which was created for the very purpose of existing and living a life naturally suited to it, since the cause itself is bound up with its nature, and is recognised only in connection with existence itself, can never admit of any cause which shall utterly annihilate its existence.

18. But since this cause is seen to lie in perpetual existence, the being so created must be preserved for ever, doing and

® 2016 apostle Arne Horn

experiencing what is suitable to its nature, each of the two parts of which it consists contributing what belongs to it.

19. So that the soul may exist and remain without change in the nature in which it was made, and discharge its appropriate functions (*such as presiding over the impulses of the body, and judging of and measuring that which occurs from time to time by the proper standards and measures*), and the body be moved according to its nature towards its appropriate objects, and undergo the changes allotted to it, and, among the rest (*relating to age, or appearance, or size*), the resurrection.

20. For the resurrection is a species of change, and the last of all, and a change for the better of what still remains in existence at that time.

® 2016 apostle Arne Horn

Chapter 13:1-8

Continuation of the argument.

1. Confident of these things, no less than of those which have already come to pass, and reflecting on our own nature, we are content with a life associated with neediness and corruption, as suited to our present state of existence, and we steadfastly hope for a continuance of being in immortality.
2. And this we do not take without foundation from the inventions of men, feeding ourselves on false hopes, but our belief rests on a most infallible guarantee—the purpose of Him who fashioned us, according to which He made man of an immortal soul and a body, and furnished him with understanding and an innate law for the preservation and safeguard of the things given by Him as suitable to an intelligent existence and a rational life.
3. For we know well that He would not have fashioned such a being, and furnished him with everything belonging to perpetuity, had He not intended that what was so created should continue in perpetuity.
4. If, therefore, the Maker of this universe made man with a view to his partaking of an intelligent life, and that, having become a spectator of His grandeur, and of the wisdom which is manifest in all things.
5. He might continue always in the contemplation of these; then, according to the purpose of his Author, and the nature which he has received, the cause of his creation is a pledge of his continuance for ever, and this continuance is a pledge of the resurrection, without which man could not continue.
6. So that, from what has been said, it is quite clear that the resurrection is plainly proved by the cause of man's creation, and the purpose of Him who made him.
7. Such being the nature of the cause for which man has been brought into this world, the next thing will be to consider that which immediately follows, naturally or in the order proposed; and in our investigation the cause of their creation is followed by the nature of the men so created, and the nature of those created by the just judgment of their Maker upon them, and all these by the end of their existence.
8. Having investigated therefore the point placed first in order, we must now go on to consider the nature of men.

® 2016 apostle Arne Horn

Chapter 14:1-11

The resurrection does not rest solely on the fact of a future judgment.

1. The proof of the several doctrines of which the truth consists, or of any matter whatsoever proposed for examination, if it is to produce an unwavering confidence in what is said, must begin, not from anything without, nor from what certain persons think or have thought, but from the common and natural notion of the matter, or from the connection of secondary truths with primary ones.
2. For the question relates either to primary beliefs, and then all that is necessary is reminiscence, so as to stir up the natural notion; or to things which naturally follow from the first and to their natural sequence.
3. And in these things we must observe order, showing what strictly follows from the first truths, or from those which are placed first, so as neither to be unmindful of the truth, or of our certainty respecting it, nor to confound the things arranged by nature and distinguished from each other, or break up the natural order.
4. Hence I think it behoves those who desire to handle the subject with fairness, and who wish to form an intelligent judgment whether there is a resurrection or not, first to consider attentively the force of the arguments contributing to the proof of this, and what place each of them holds—which is first, which second, which third, and which last.
5. And in the arrangement of these they should place first the cause of the creation of men,—namely, the purpose of the Creator in making man.
6. And then connect with this, as is suitable, the nature of the men so created; not as being second in order, but because we are unable to pass our judgment on both at the same time, although they have the closest natural connection with each other, and are of equal force in reference to the subject before us.
7. But while from these proofs as the primary ones, and as being derived from the work of creation, the resurrection is clearly demonstrated, none the less can we gain conviction respecting it from the arguments taken from providence,—I mean from the reward or punishment due to each man in accordance with just judgment, and from the end of human existence.
8. For many, in discussing the subject of the resurrection, have

® 2016 apostle Arne Horn

rested the whole cause on the third argument alone, deeming that the cause of the resurrection is the judgment.

9. But the fallacy of this is very clearly shown, from the fact that, although all human beings who die rise again, yet not all who rise again are to be judged.

10. For if only a just judgment were the cause of the resurrection, it would of course follow that those who had done neither evil nor good—namely, very young children—would not rise again.

11. But seeing that all are to rise again, those who have died in infancy as well as others, they too justify our conclusion that the resurrection takes place not for the sake of the judgment as the primary reason, but in consequence of the purpose of God in forming men, and the nature of the beings so formed.

® 2016 apostle Arne Horn

Chapter 15:1-14

Argument for the resurrection from the nature of man.

1. But while the cause discoverable in the creation of men is of itself sufficient to prove that the resurrection follows by natural sequence on the dissolution of bodies, yet it is perhaps right not to shrink from adducing either of the proposed arguments, but, agreeably to what has been said, to point out to those who are not able of themselves to discern them, the arguments from each of the truths evolved from the primary; and first and foremost, the nature of the men created, which conducts us to the same notion, and has the same force as evidence of the resurrection.
2. For if the whole nature of men in general is composed of an immortal soul and a body which was fitted to it in the creation, and if neither to the nature of the soul by itself.
3. Nor to the nature of the body separately, has God assigned such a creation or such a life and entire course of existence as this, but to men compounded of the two, in order that they may.
4. When they have passed through their present existence, arrive at one common end, with the same elements of which they are composed at their birth and during life, it unavoidably follows, since one living-being is formed from the two, experiencing whatever the soul experiences and whatever the body experiences, doing and performing whatever requires the judgment of the senses or of the reason, that the whole series of these things must be referred to some one end, in order that they all, and by means of all,—namely, man's creation, man's nature, man's life, man's doings and sufferings, his course of existence, and the end suitable to his nature,—may concur in one harmony and the same common experience.
5. But if there is some one harmony and community of experience belonging to the whole being, whether of the things which spring from the soul or of those which are accomplished by means of the body, the end for all these must also be one.
6. And the end will be in strictness one, if the being whose end that end is remains the same in its constitution; and the being will be exactly the same, if all those things of which the being consists as parts are the same.
7. And they will be the same in respect of their peculiar union, if the parts dissolved are again united for the constitution of the

® 2016 apostle Arne Horn

being.

8. And the constitution of the same men of necessity proves that a resurrection will follow of the dead and dissolved bodies; for without this, neither could the same parts be united according to nature with one another, nor could the nature of the same men be reconstituted.

9. And if both understanding and reason have been given to men for the discernment of things which are perceived by the understanding, and not of existences only, but also of the goodness and wisdom and rectitude of their Giver, it necessarily follows that, since those things continue for the sake of which the rational judgment is given, the judgment given for these things should also continue.

10. But it is impossible for this to continue, unless the nature which has received it, and in which it adheres, continues. But that which has received both understanding and reason is man, not the soul by itself.

11. Man, therefore, who consists of the two parts, must continue for ever. But it is impossible for him to continue unless he rise again.

12. For if no resurrection were to take place, the nature of men as men would not continue. And if the nature of men does not continue, in vain has the soul been fitted to the need of the body and to its experiences; in vain has the body been fettered so that it cannot obtain what it longs for, obedient to the reins of the soul, and guided by it as with a bridle; in vain is the understanding, in vain is wisdom.

13. And the observance of rectitude, or even the practice of every virtue, and the enactment and enforcement of laws,—to say all in a word, whatever is noble in men or for men's sake, or rather the very creation and nature of men.

14. But if vanity is utterly excluded from all the works of God, and from all the gifts bestowed by Him, the conclusion is unavoidable, that, along with the interminable duration of the soul, there will be a perpetual continuance of the body according to its proper nature.

® 2016 apostle Arne Horn

Chapter 16:1-9

Analogy of death and sleep, and consequent argument for the resurrection.

1. And let no one think it strange that we call by the name of life a continuance of being which is interrupted by death and corruption; but let him consider rather that this word has not one meaning only, nor is there only one measure of continuance, because the nature also of the things that continue is not one.
2. For if each of the things that continue has its continuance according to its peculiar nature, neither in the case of those who are wholly incorruptible and immortal shall we find the continuance like ours, because the natures of superior beings do not take the level of such as are inferior.
3. Nor in men is it proper to look for a continuance invariable and unchangeable; inasmuch as the former are from the first created immortal, and continue to exist without end by the simple will of their Maker, and men, in respect of the soul, have from their first origin an unchangeable continuance, but in respect of the body obtain immortality by means of change.
4. This is what is meant by the doctrine of the resurrection; and, looking to this, we both await the dissolution of the body, as the sequel to a life of want and corruption, and after this we hope for a continuance with immortality.
5. Not putting either our death on a level with the death of the irrational animals, or the continuance of man with the continuance of immortals, lest we should unawares in this way put human nature and life on a level with things with which it is not proper to compare them.
6. It ought not, therefore, to excite dissatisfaction, if some inequality appears to exist in regard to the duration of men; nor, because the separation of the soul from the members of the body and the dissolution of its parts interrupts the continuity of life, must we therefore despair of the resurrection.
7. For although the relaxation of the senses and of the physical powers, which naturally takes place in sleep, seems to interrupt the sensational life when men sleep at equal intervals of time, and, as it were, come back to life again, yet we do not refuse to call it life; and for this reason.
8. I suppose, some call sleep the brother of death, not as deriving their origin from the same ancestors and fathers, but because those who are dead and those who sleep are subject

® 2016 apostle Arne Horn

to similar states, as regards at least the stillness and the absence of all sense of the present or the past, or rather of existence itself and their own life.

9. If, therefore, we do not refuse to call by the name of life the life of men full of such inequality from birth to dissolution, and interrupted by all those things which we have before mentioned, neither ought we to despair of the life succeeding to dissolution, such as involves the resurrection, although for a time it is interrupted by the separation of the soul from the body.

® 2016 apostle Arne Horn

Chapter 17:1-6

The series of changes we can now trace in man renders a resurrection probable.

1. For this nature of men, which has inequality allotted to it from the first, and according to the purpose of its Maker, has an unequal life and continuance, interrupted sometimes by sleep, at another time by death, and by the changes incident to each period of life, whilst those which follow the first are not clearly seen beforehand.
2. Would any one have believed, unless taught by experience, that in the soft seed alike in all its parts there was deposited such a variety and number of great powers, or of masses, which in this way arise and become consolidated—I mean of bones, and nerves, and cartilages, of muscles too, and flesh, and intestines, and the other parts of the body?
3. For neither in the yet moist seed is anything of this kind to be seen, nor even in infants do any of those things make their appearance which pertain to adults, or in the adult period what belongs to those who are past their prime, or in these what belongs to such as have grown old.
4. But although some of the things I have said exhibit not at all, and others but faintly, the natural sequence and the changes that come upon the nature of men, yet all who are not blinded in their judgment of these matters by vice or sloth, know that there must be first the depositing of the seed.
5. And that when this is completely organized in respect of every member and part and the progeny comes forth to the light, there comes the growth belonging to the first period of life, and the maturity which attends growth, and after the maturity the slackening of the physical powers till old age, and then, when the body is worn out, its dissolution.
6. As, therefore, in this matter, though neither the seed has inscribed upon it the life or form of men, nor the life the dissolution into the primary elements; the succession of natural occurrences makes things credible which have no credibility from the phenomena themselves, much more does reason, tracing out the truth from the natural sequence, afford ground for believing in the resurrection, since it is safer and stronger than experience for establishing the truth.

® 2016 apostle Arne Horn

Chapter 18:1-17

Judgment must have reference both to soul and body: there will therefore be a resurrection.

1. The arguments I just now proposed for examination, as establishing the truth of the resurrection, are all of the same kind, since they all start from the same point; for their starting-point is the origin of the first men by creation.
2. But while some of them derive their strength from the starting-point itself from which they take their rise, others, consequent upon the nature and the life of men, acquire their credibility from the superintendence of God over us.
3. For the cause according to which, and on account of which, men have come into being, being closely connected with the nature of men, derives its force from creation.
4. But the argument from rectitude, which represents God as judging men according as they have lived well or ill, derives its force from the end of their existence: they come into being on the former ground, but their state depends more on God's superintendence.
5. And now that the matters which come first have been demonstrated by me to the best of my ability, it will be well to prove our proposition by those also which come after—I mean by the reward or punishment due to each man in accordance with righteous judgment, and by the final cause of human existence.
6. And of these I put foremost that which takes the lead by nature, and inquire first into the argument relating to the judgment: premising only one thing, from concern for the principle which appertains to the matters before us.
7. And for order—namely, that it is incumbent on those who admit God to be the Maker of this universe, to ascribe to His wisdom and rectitude the preservation and care of all that has been created, if they wish to keep to their own principles.
8. And with such views to hold that nothing either in earth or in heaven is without guardianship or providence, but that, on the contrary, to everything, invisible and visible alike, small and great, the attention of the Creator reaches; for all created things require the attention of the Creator.
9. And each one in particular, according to its nature and the end for which it was made: though I think it would be a useless expenditure of trouble to go through the list now, or distinguish between the several cases, or mention in detail what is suitable to each nature.

® 2016 apostle Arne Horn

10. Man, at all events, of whom it is now our business to speak, as being in want, requires food; as being mortal, posterity; as being rational, a process of judgment.

11. But if each of these things belongs to man by nature, and he requires food for his life, and requires posterity for the continuance of the race, and requires a judgment in order that food and posterity may be according to law, it of course follows, since food and posterity refer to both together, that the judgment must be referred to them too (*by both together I mean man, consisting of soul and body*).

12. And that such man becomes accountable for all his actions, and receives for them either reward or punishment. Now, if the righteous judgment awards to both together its retribution for the deeds wrought.

13. And if it is not proper that either the soul alone should receive the wages of the deeds wrought in union with the body (*for this of itself has no inclination to the faults which are committed in connection with the pleasure or food and culture of the body*), or that the body alone should (*for this of itself is incapable of distinguishing law and justice*).

14. But man, composed of these, is subjected to trial for each of the deeds wrought by him; and if reason does not find this happening either in this life *(for the award according to merit finds no place in the present existence, since many atheists and persons who practice every iniquity and wickedness live on to the last, unvisited by calamity, whilst, on the contrary, those who have manifestly lived an exemplary life in respect of every virtue, live in pain, in insult, in calumny and outrage, and suffering of all kinds*).

15. Or after death (*for both together no longer exist, the soul being separated from the body, and the body itself being resolved again into the materials out of which it was composed, and no longer retaining anything of its former structure or form, much less the remembrance of its actions*).

16. The result of all this is very plain to every one,—namely, that, in the language of the apostle, this corruptible (*and dissoluble*) must put on incorruption, in order that those who were dead, having been made alive by the resurrection.

17. And the parts that were separated and entirely dissolved having been again united, each one may, in accordance with justice, receive what he has done by the body, whether it be good or bad.

 ® 2016 apostle Arne Horn

Chapter 19:1-13

Man would be more unfavourably situated than the beasts if there were no resurrection.

1. In replying, then, to those who acknowledge a divine superintendence, and admit the same principles as we do, yet somehow depart from their own admissions, one may use such arguments as those which have been adduced.
2. And many more than these, should he be disposed to amplify what has been said only concisely and in a cursory manner.
3. But in dealing with those who differ from us concerning primary truths, it will perhaps be well to lay down another principle antecedent to these, joining with them in doubting of the things to which their opinions relate, and examining the matter along with them in this manner—whether the life of men.
4. And their entire course of existence, is overlooked, and a sort of dense darkness is poured down upon the earth, hiding in ignorance and silence both the men themselves and their actions; or whether it is much safer to be of opinion that the Maker presides over the things which He Himself has made, inspecting all things whatsoever which exist, or come into existence, Judge of both deeds and purposes.
5. For if no judgment whatever were to be passed on the actions of men, men would have no advantage over the irrational creatures, but rather would fare worse than these do, inasmuch as they keep in subjection their passions.
6. And concern themselves about piety, and righteousness, and the other virtues; and a life after the manner of brutes would be the best, virtue would be absurd, the threat of judgment a matter for broad laughter, indulgence in every kind of pleasure the highest good, and the common resolve of all these and their one law would be that maxim, so dear to the intemperate and lewd, *"Let us eat and drink, for to-morrow we die."*
7. For the termination of such a life is not even pleasure, as some suppose, but utter insensibility.
8. But if the Maker of men takes any concern about His own works, and the distinction is anywhere to be found between those who have lived well and ill, it must be either in the present life, while men are still living who have conducted themselves virtuously or viciously.
9. Or after death, when men are in a state of separation and dissolution. But according to neither of these suppositions can

® 2016 apostle Arne Horn

we find a just judgment taking place; for neither do the good in the present life obtain the rewards of virtue, nor yet do the bad receive the wages of vice.

10. I pass over the fact, that so long as the nature we at present possess is preserved, the moral nature is not able to bear a punishment commensurate with the more numerous or more serious faults.

11. For the robber, or ruler, or tyrant, who has unjustly put to death myriads on myriads, could not by one death make restitution for these deeds; and the man who holds no true opinion concerning God.

12. But lives in all outrage and blasphemy, despises divine things, breaks the laws, commits outrage against boys and women alike, razes cities unjustly, burns houses with their inhabitants, and devastates a country, and at the same time destroys inhabitants of cities and peoples, and even an entire nation—how in a mortal body could he endure a penalty adequate to these crimes, since death prevents the deserved punishment, and the mortal nature does not suffice for any single one of his deeds?

13. It is proved, therefore, that neither in the present life is there a judgment according to men's deserts, nor after death.

 ® 2016 apostle Arne Horn

Chapter 20:1-5

Man must be possessed both of a body and soul hereafter, that the judgment passed upon him may be just.

1. For either death is the entire extinction of life, the soul being dissolved and corrupted along with the body, or the soul remains by itself, incapable of dissolution, of dispersion, of corruption, whilst the body is corrupted and dissolved, retaining no longer any remembrance of past actions, nor sense of what it experienced in connection with the soul.
2. If the life of men is to be utterly extinguished, it is manifest there will be no care for men who are not living, no judgment respecting those who have lived in virtue or in vice; but there will rush in again upon us whatever belongs to a lawless life, and the swarm of absurdities which follow from it, and that which is the summit of this lawlessness—atheism.
3. But if the body were to be corrupted, and each of the dissolved particles to pass to its kindred element, yet the soul to remain by itself as immortal, neither on this supposition would any judgment on the soul take place, since there would be an absence of equity.
4. For it is unlawful to suspect that any judgment can proceed out of God and from God which is wanting in equity. Yet equity is wanting to the judgment, if the being is not preserved in existence who practiced righteousness or lawlessness: for that which practiced each of the things in life on which the judgment is passed was man, not soul by itself.
5. To sum up all in a word, this view will in no case consist with equity.

® 2016 apostle Arne Horn

Chapter 21:1-10

Continuation of the argument.

1. For if good deeds are rewarded, the body will clearly be wronged, inasmuch as it has shared with the soul in the toils connected with well-doing, but does not share in the reward of the good deeds, and because, though the soul is often excused for certain faults on the ground of the body's neediness and want, the body itself is deprived of all share in the good deeds done, the toils on behalf of which it helped to bear during life.
2. Nor, again, if faults are judged, is the soul dealt fairly with, supposing it alone to pay the penalty for the faults it committed through being solicited by the body and drawn away by it to its own appetites and motions, at one time being seized upon and carried off, at another attracted in some very violent manner, and sometimes concurring with it by way of kindness and attention to its preservation.
3. How can it possibly be other than unjust for the soul to be judged by itself in respect of things towards which in its own nature it feels no appetite, no motion, no impulse, such as licentiousness, violence, covetousness, injustice, and the unjust acts arising out of these?
4. For if the majority of such evils come from men's not having the mastery of the passions which solicit them, and they are solicited by the neediness and want of the body, and the care and attention required by it (*for these are the motives for every acquisition of property, and especially for the using of it. and moreover for marriage and all the actions of life, in which things, and in connection with which, is seen what is faulty and what is not so*).
5. How can it be just for the soul alone to be judged in respect of those things which the body is the first to be sensible of, and in which it draws the soul away to sympathy and participation in actions with a view to things which it wants.
6. And that the appetites and pleasures, and moreover the fears and sorrows, in which whatever exceeds the proper bounds is amenable to judgment, should be set in motion by the body, and yet that the sins arising from these, and the punishments for the sins committed, should fall upon the soul alone, which neither needs anything of this sort, nor desires nor fears or suffers of itself any such thing as man is wont to suffer?
7. But even if we hold that these affections do not pertain to the body alone, but to man, in saying which we should speak

® 2016 apostle Arne Horn

correctly, because the life of man is one, though composed of the two, yet surely we shall not assert that these things belong to the soul, if we only look simply at its peculiar nature.

8. For if it is absolutely without need of food, it can never desire those things which it does not in the least require for its subsistence; nor can it feel any impulse towards any of those things which it is not at all fitted to use; nor, again, can it be grieved at the want of money or other property, since these are not suited to it.

9. And if, too, it is superior to corruption, it fears nothing whatever as destructive of itself: it has no dread of famine, or disease, or mutilation, or blemish, or fire, or sword, since it cannot suffer from any of these any hurt or pain, because neither bodies nor bodily powers touch it at all.

10. But if it is absurd to attach the passions to the soul as belonging specially to it, it is in the highest degree unjust and unworthy of the judgment of God to lay upon the soul alone the sins which spring from them, and the consequent punishments.

 ® 2016 apostle Arne Horn

Chapter 22:1-7

Continuation of the argument.

1. In addition to what has been said, is it not absurd that, while we cannot even have the notion of virtue and vice as existing separately in the soul (*for we recognise the virtues as man's virtues, even as in like manner vice, their opposite, as not belonging to the soul in separation from the body, and existing by itself*), yet that the reward or punishment for these should be assigned to the soul alone?
2. How can any one have even the notion of courage or fortitude as existing in the soul alone, when it has no fear of death, or wounds, or maiming, or loss, or maltreatment, or of the pain connected with these, or the suffering resulting from them?
3. And what shall we say of self-control and temperance, when there is no desire drawing it to food or sexual intercourse, or other pleasures and enjoyments, nor any other thing soliciting it from within or exciting it from without?
4. And what of practical wisdom, when things are not proposed to it which may or may not be done, nor things to be chosen or avoided, or rather when there is in it no motion at all or natural impulse towards the doing of anything?
5. And how in any sense can equity be an attribute of souls, either in reference to one another or to anything else, whether of the same or of a different kind, when they are not able from any source, or by any means, or in any way, to bestow that which is equal according to merit or according to analogy, with the exception of the honour rendered to God.
6. And, moreover, have no impulse or motion towards the use of their own things, or abstinence from those of others, since the use of those things which are according to nature, or the abstinence from them, is considered in reference to those who are so constituted as to use them, whereas the soul neither wants anything.
7. Nor is so constituted as to use any things or any single thing, and therefore what is called the independent action of the parts cannot be found in the soul so constituted?

® 2016 apostle Arne Horn

Chapter 23:1-8

Continuation of the argument.

1. But the most irrational thing of all is this: to impose properly sanctioned laws on men, and then to assign to their souls alone the recompense of their lawful or unlawful deeds.
2. For if he who receives the laws would also justly receive the recompense of the transgression of the laws, and if it was man that received the laws, and not the soul by itself, man must also bear the recompense for the sins committed, and not the soul by itself, since God has not enjoined on souls to abstain from things which have no relation to them, such as adultery, murder, theft, rapine, dishonour to parents, and every desire in general that tends to the injury and loss of our neighbours.
3. For neither the command, *"Honour thy father and thy mother,"* is adapted to souls alone, since such names are not applicable to them, for souls do not produce souls, so as to appropriate the appellation of father or mother, but men produce men.
4. Nor could the command, *"Thou shalt not commit adultery,"* ever be properly addressed to souls, or even thought of in such a connection, since the difference of male and female does not exist in them, nor any aptitude for sexual intercourse, nor appetite for it.
5. And where there is no appetite, there can be no intercourse; and where there is no intercourse at all, there can be no legitimate intercourse, namely marriage; and where there is no lawful intercourse, neither can there be unlawful desire of, or intercourse with, another man's wife, namely adultery.
6. Nor, again, is the prohibition of theft, or of the desire of having more, applicable to souls, for they do not need those things, through the need of which, by reason of natural indigence or want, men are accustomed to steal or to rob, such as gold, or silver, or an animal, or something else adapted for food, or shelter, or use.
7. For to an immortal nature everything which is desired by the needy as useful is useless. But let the fuller discussion of these matters be left to those who wish to investigate each point more exactly, or to contend more earnestly with opponents.
8. But, since what has just been said, and that which concurs with this to guarantee the resurrection, suffices for us, it would not be seasonable to dwell any longer upon them; for

® 2016 apostle Arne Horn

we have not made it our aim to omit nothing that might be said, but to point out in a summary manner to those who have assembled what ought to be thought concerning the resurrection, and to adapt to the capacity of those present the arguments bearing on this question.

 ® 2016 apostle Arne Horn

Chapter 24:1-6

Argument for the resurrection from the chief end of man.

1. The points proposed for consideration having been to some extent investigated, it remains to examine the argument from the end or final cause, which indeed has already emerged in what has been said, and only requires just so much attention and further discussion as may enable us to avoid the appearance of leaving unmentioned any of the matters briefly referred to by us, and thus indirectly damaging the subject or the division of topics made at the outset.
2. For the sake of those present, therefore, and of others who may pay attention to this subject, it may be well just to signify that each of those things which are constituted by nature, and of those which are made by art, must have an end peculiar to itself, as indeed is taught us by the common sense of all men, and testified by the things that pass before our eyes.
3. For do we not see that husbandmen have one end, and physicians another; and again, the things which spring out of the earth another, and the animals nourished upon it, and produced according to a certain natural series, another?
4. If this is evident, and natural and artificial powers, and the actions arising from these, must by all means be accompanied by an end in accordance with nature, it is absolutely necessary that the end of men, since it is that of a peculiar nature, should be separated from community with the rest; for it is not lawful to suppose the same end for beings destitute of rational judgment, and of those whose actions are regulated by the innate law and reason, and who live an intelligent life and observe justice.
5. Freedom from pain, therefore, cannot be the proper end for the latter, for this they would have in common with beings utterly devoid of sensibility: nor can it consist in the enjoyment of things which nourish or delight the body, or in an abundance of pleasures; else a life like that of the brutes must hold the first place, while that regulated by virtue is without a final cause.
6. For such an end as this, I suppose, belongs to beasts and cattle, not to men possessed of an immortal soul and rational judgment.

 ® 2016 apostle Arne Horn

Chapter 25:1-7

Argument continued and concluded.

1. Nor again is it the happiness of soul separated from body: for we are not inquiring about the life or final cause of either of the parts of which man consists, but of the being who is composed of both; for such is every man who has a share in this present existence, and there must be some appropriate end proposed for this life.
2. But if it is the end of both parts together, and this can be discovered neither while they are still living in the present state of existence through the numerous causes already mentioned.
3. Nor yet when the soul is in a state of separation, because the man cannot be said to exist when the body is dissolved, and indeed entirely scattered abroad, even though the soul continue by itself—it is absolutely necessary that the end of a man's being should appear in some reconstitution of the two together, and of the same living being.
4. And as this follows of necessity, there must by all means be a resurrection of the bodies which are dead, or even entirely dissolved, and the same men must be formed anew, since the law of nature ordains the end not absolutely, nor as the end of any men whatsoever, but of the same men who passed through the previous life; but it is impossible for the same men to be reconstituted unless the same bodies are restored to the same souls.
5. But that the same soul should obtain the same body is impossible in any other way, and possible only by the resurrection; for if this takes place, an end befitting the nature of men follows also.
6. And we shall make no mistake in saying, that the final cause of an intelligent life and rational judgment, is to be occupied uninterruptedly with those objects to which the natural reason is chiefly and primarily adapted, and to delight unceasingly in the contemplation of **Him who is** and of His decrees, notwithstanding that the majority of men, because they are affected too passionately and too violently by things below, pass through life without attaining this object.
7. For the large number of those who fail of the end that belongs to them does not make void the common lot, since the examination relates to individuals, and the reward or punishment of lives ill or well spent is proportioned to the merit of each.

® 2016 apostle Arne Horn

® 2016 apostle Arne Horn

 ® 2016 apostle Arne Horn

® 2016 apostle Arne Horn

® 2016 apostle Arne Horn

www.ingramcontent.com/pod-product-compliance
Ingram Content Group UK Ltd.
Pitfield, Milton Keynes, MK11 3LW, UK
UKHW041836200726
13854UKWH00003BA/1159